# Zoe's Win

## Jane Colby

**Dome Vision**

Published by:

Dome Vision,
Rodmans Hoppett, Ongar Road, Fyfield, Essex CM5 0RB

ISBN 0 9537330 0 9

Design, typesetting & production: Country Books, Little Longstone, Derbyshire DE45 1NN

Printed & Bound by: MFP Design & Print, Stretford, Manchester M32 0JT

# Dedication

This book is dedicated to all young people with ME, with my admiration. I have read everything you sent me and will publish more in the future.

# CONTENTS

## PART 1

## PART 2

It is hoped that the ME-friendly typeface chosen for Part 1
will facilitate its use by young people with ME.

# PART 1

# Zoe's Win

"Pull yourself together, girl! You're always fussing about something. There's nothing wrong with you. You can't win if you don't try."

"I am trying, Sir."

"Try a bit harder, then."

And Mr Fisher grins at me, willing me on. All he wants is for me to do my best. All I want is for me to do my best. But I'm already trying as hard as I can, running, pushing, driving myself on.

My feet sound hollow somehow, thud-thudding on the hard ground, jarring my whole body. And thud-thud again, like a great echo in my brain.

"Come on, Zoe, work at it, give it some welly."

That's always Mr Fisher's way of putting it. What does it mean, anyway?

I can hardly answer, I'm just panting. And I'm not getting anywhere, it's as if I was made of lead.

Why won't my body do what I tell it? The whole class are ahead of me now. I don't think I'm even going to make it round the field. Oh, this is really stupid.

Mr Fisher's voice softens.

"You can do it, Zoe," he says, running beside me in the hot sunshine. "You don't want Gary beating you, do you?"

"No, Sir."

"Well, come on then."

So we run together, my PE teacher and I, we slog on between the white lines of the track and the sun beats down on our heads and the sweat rolls into my eyes and I feel unreal. I'm not here, my body is here but I'm not.

I won't let Gary beat me, though. I'll overtake. I've done it before. I'm supposed to be representing the school soon.

*Run Zoe run Zoe run Zoe run . . .*
Make it have a rhythm
Say it in your mind
*Run Zoe run Zoe run Zoe run . . .*

I'll show them, I'll show them all. I'll get there if it kills me, it doesn't matter if it hurts. And it does hurt. Why does it hurt so much?

What's happening?

Why do my legs feel so heavy?

"Sir! Sir, there's something wrong with Zoe."

"Zoe? You OK?"

Lynne's bending over me.

Why am I lying here? Did I fall down?

Mr Fisher's bending over me too.

What's he saying? I can see his mouth moving, asking me something. But I can't seem to understand.

My heart's beating so fast I feel as if it's going to blow up.

"Did she faint?"

"I don't know what happened. One minute she was running – the next she just collapsed."

"Don't cry, Zoe."

"I'm not crying!"

But look, I am crying, I can feel tears on my face. And I'm shaking.

I think I'm cold. Shivery, like the flu.

That's it. I've caught that summer flu. That's all it is . . .

Lynne's putting her arm round me, they're trying to help me up. My arms and legs have gone like water, all the energy running away out of them. There's nothing of me left.

"It's the heat. Take her inside."

Mr Fisher's quite kind really. He just likes us all to do well.

Someone's giving me a glass of water. What's this chair they're sitting me on?

"Lynne! Don't leave me alone, don't go away!"

Was that my voice? It sounds so loud. Am I shouting? I'm frightened. They mustn't leave me alone, they mustn't. I feel so ill, terribly, terribly ill. What's happening to me? This isn't what illness feels like – am I going to die?

"Zoe? I've got to go. We're having another practice. It's Sports Day tomorrow, remember? They want me back again. Zoe?"

"No don't, please. Just stay till I feel a bit better . . . something awful's happening to me. Something awful."

"What do you mean? What's happening?"

"I don't know what I mean. It's just – something really bad."

11

"No, it's not. Mr Fisher says it's just the heat."

"It's not just the heat, Lynne. I'm really ill, I know I am. I couldn't move out there. I couldn't run. I've never felt like this in my life."

Lynne's staring at me with a very funny expression on her face.

"Here's Mrs Wood now. She'll look after you. Look, I've got to go."

I'm crying again. I don't want Mrs Wood. I want Lynne. I want mum. No-one's listening to me. No-one's listening.

I've missed Sports Day.

The blue team lost. They weren't too pleased, they always depend on me. But I couldn't help it, I didn't even know what day it was!

Now of course, I'm stuck at home, in bed. No-one seems to know what's wrong.

The doctor came. "Maybe she's got a bug," he said to mum. "She'll be all right in a few days."

But that was weeks ago. I ache and ache, my neck's all stiff, my head's throbbing, I feel sick. I keep falling asleep but they wake me up again, they talk to each other and don't seem to hear what I'm saying. Why can't they just let me sleep it off?

"Come down and have lunch, Zoe. It'll do you good to get out of bed."

That's my mum calling. She's had to take some time off work to look after me. She wants me to get better soon in case they give her job to somebody else.

I'd better go downstairs, she's calling again.

"It's only soup and toast, Zoe. You can manage that, surely?"

I don't feel like soup and toast. I don't feel like any-thing. But I know I've got to eat. Everyone says I'm getting thin. And I am.

"Come on, dear. It's all ready."

Oh, well.

I'm swinging my legs over the side of the bed now – they seem to weigh tons. OK I've got my feet flat on the floor . . . my legs will hardly support me. This is stupid. I'm a *runner*, and I'm going to be a marathon runner, but my legs will hardly support me! Some runner. I feel really weird. Wobbly, quivery . . .

Whoops. I just saved myself on the doorhandle.

I'm at the top of the stairs now. Right; I've made it so far.

How do I get downstairs? I can't seem to remember which foot to put first.

"Ah, here you are Zoe. I was just coming up. How are you feeling?"

"I've got a pain."

"Where?"

"Everywhere. All of me seems to hurt."

"Well, don't just stand there. Come down."

It's no good. I can't remember what to do. Perhaps if I put my left foot on the first step – now I'll put the right one down past it. Oh, no! It's all gone wrong. My knees are giving way.

"Zoe!"

I can hear mum calling out from somewhere.

"Mum!"

I'm at the bottom of the stairs. I don't remember falling at all, but I'm right at the bottom. I don't think I've hurt myself . . . but what are my legs doing? I feel as if I'm wired up to a battery and all the bits of my legs are twitching out of time with one another. Like someone's set off a sparkler inside.

"Oh my goodness – are you all right?"

Mum's staring down at me. It's just like when I fell on the field. Everyone stared at me then, too.

"It's OK mum, I'm fine."

Why did I say that? I'm not fine at all.

"You gave me such a fright. You really must be more careful. Now stand up slowly and don't rush. The soup's getting cold." She turns back to the kitchen again. "Really, you *must* be more careful. Promise me now, I've got to go into the office this afternoon."

So I promise. I can hardly get my body off the floor. How on earth can I make mum understand what it feels like? I don't understand it myself.

Anyway, I'm standing up. I've managed to do that.

Mum's gone back into the kitchen, she's banging plates about.

"It's potato and leek. Nice and filling. I'll have some with you, to keep you company. I've kept the toast warm, like you like it."

I feel awful. I feel really awful. I shouldn't have got out of bed. I've only been out of bed a few minutes and it's wiped me out.

When you're having a nightmare do you ever try to wake yourself up? I keep trying to wake myself up. This just isn't real.

Now what? It's my face. Something's happened to my face.

"Mum! Mum!"

I'm scared.

Mum comes rushing out again. She looks as scared as me.

"What? What is it?"

"My face. I can't feel my face – I can't feel it, Mum! All down the left side, it's just gone numb."

"What do you mean, you can't feel it?"

"Well, I can sort of half feel it. Not properly though. I can't describe it – it's like if I'd been to the dentist and had an injection – it's like when it's wearing off."

"I'll get the doctor. You sit down, Zoe."

So I do sit down. What a relief, just to sit. To support my body and lean it on something.

Mum's on the telephone trying to make the woman at the surgery believe I need a doctor.

I suppose I'd better try and eat this soup.

You know what soup looks like when it gets cold? All sort of sick colour and full of lumps? The lumps are only potatoes really, but they look disgusting.

I'm going to be sick . . .

"No, I can't get her to the surgery – she's not strong enough – look I've got to go, she's being sick again – Zoe, wait till I'm off the phone . . ."

I won't be sick, I won't. I'll have a bite of toast.

The toast tastes like sawdust, it's so hard to chew. It's making my jaw ache. I never knew it took so much energy to chew. I'm getting breathless too.

"I can't eat this, mum. I just can't."

I can see myself in the kitchen mirror. My face is a horrible colour, like dough that hasn't been cooked. And all down one side it *feels* like a lump of dough, not skin at all. And now my left eyelid's twitching too, just like my legs.

Oh, *what?* I've knocked the soup bowl onto the floor. Oh, yuk. What a mess.

"Zoe!" says mum in despair.

She looks at the sloppy muck spreading over the floor. We stare at one another in the middle of it all. We don't know whether to laugh or cry. In the end we laugh.

"What *else* can go wrong? You'd better not try to do anything at all or you'll wreck the whole place."

We both start to laugh properly then, but it makes me breathless again so I stop.

"I'm sorry. I'll help you clear it up."

But I can't do that either. Mum can see I look dreadful. I think she's trying not to let me see how scared she is.

"The doctor's coming when he can. You haven't combed your hair."

"I haven't got the strength. I'm sorry."

"Never mind. I'll do it for you."

And so she has to comb my hair. I can't even comb my hair. I'm disgusted with myself. Really angry.

But my mum's really kind. She combs my hair gently, so gently. I wish everyone was kind like that.

And I wish I understood what's happening. How long am I going to be like this and will it get any worse?

"Hi, Zoe."

I've hardly seen my friends since last term. I've been stuck in the house. But now it's a new term, and everyone's milling around waiting to go inside.

Gary looks me up and down as if he thinks I'm going to collapse again.

"You've been away ages. Are you OK?" He grins. "Mr Fisher's keeping your place in the team for you."

I know why he's grinning. He just wants to beat me again.

I bet you're surprised I'm back at school after being so ill. But I am. It just went away. All the aches and pains. I couldn't believe it. I'd started to think they would never go, but they just did. It's great to see all my friends again.

"Zoe!"

Lynne. I've missed her most of all. She came to see me once but then she got busy and I haven't seen her since.

"Hi."

"I like your hair."

"Thanks. Mum let me have it cut like this."

"Coming round after school? I've got War of the Titans version 3."

"What's that?"

Lynne stares at me.

"Where've you been, Zoe?"

I try not to feel stupid.

"I haven't been keeping up. I'm only just OK to come back . . . I've been sleeping a lot," I add, as a sort of apology.

"You mean you've been ill all the holiday?"

"I'm better now though. All my pains have gone. It was just some virus. I had to rest in bed for *ages.*"

"How long?"

"Tell you later – what's Miss Everett like?"

I don't want to talk about being ill – I'd rather just forget it. Miss Everett's our new class teacher. I haven't met her yet. That's what I really want to know about.

"She's OK."

It's the best day to get back to school. We've got swimming and I haven't been swimming for months. Miss Everett's taking us on the bus. We have to leave really early, before school starts. Mr Fisher won't be there till later.

I love swimming. It's another thing I win at. The bus ride isn't long because we use the pool in the centre of town. It's a full size pool. The water seems to smell very strong today. It's just lying there, a really brilliant blue, swaying slightly, with the dark painted lines not quite straight at the bottom.

"In you go, Zoe."

I'm going to do my best – I'm going to show them all that I'm really back and they'd better reckon with a bit of strong competition for a change.

My legs feel a bit wobbly of course. I'm not fit yet. But when I exercise them they'll get stronger.

We crash through the smooth surface like bombs, sending up spouts of spray. My favourite stroke is the crawl. And I swim well on my back too. I count the beams in the ceiling so I know exactly when to turn at the end of the bath.

I'm going to do three lengths straight off.

"Well done, Zoe," Miss Everett's calling from the side. "Keep up your stroke, keep the rhythm. That's it."

Gary's behind me. I can remember when he beat me at running, all that time ago. Ha. I'll teach him. It feels so good sweeping my arms through the water, feeling it pushed away behind me, shooting me forwards. I'm a bit weak, though. I need to practice hard.

"Come on, Zoe!"

Lynne is egging me on from the other end. Mr Fisher doesn't let us call out, but Miss Everett doesn't seem to mind.

"Ga-ry! Ga-ry! Ga-ry! Ga-ry!"

That's Gary's lot trying to get him to overtake. But he's not going to overtake me . Not this time.

I can hear him splashing behind me. His fingers are there, just the tips of his fingers, I can see them every time I turn my head to breathe. He's gaining on me, catching up.

"Ga-ry! Ga-ry! Ga-ry!"

They're chanting like a football crowd.

And Gary's coming on, I can see the whole of his arm now. I'm dropping back. Back, back . . . Why am I stopping?

It's my heart again, thudding and thudding inside my chest. I feel dizzy . . .

But I can't stop, not here, I'm in the deep end. There's no grass to fall down on here . . .

*Help!*

I want to cry out but I can't, I've no breath.

*Help!*

The water's closing over my head, I've taken a great mouthful of it.

I'm going down, I can't seem to float properly, I can see the dark lines waving at the bottom of the pool . . .

Down, down, down . . .

"OK, Zoe, I've got you."

It's Mr Fisher. I'm not sure what's happened . . . somehow he's lifted me up to the surface – I'm grabbing onto him but I can't seem to get a grip. I'm so tired. My heart's still throbbing.

"Let go, Zoe, relax. I've got you."

Mr Fisher's strong, he's so strong. I can just let go and he'll pull me to the side and lift me out.

I'm lying on the side now. It's hard and cold. I want to get up but nothing in my body will let me.

I'm coughing, coughing up water and trying to say thank you to Mr Fisher but I can't speak.

It's happening again. It's happening all over again. I can't bear it. Why is this happening to me?

The doctor's smiling. Her name's Draycott. She's very patient, very kind. She's a specialist in what's wrong with me. I can't believe we've found someone who really understands.

"She's just done a bit too much and made herself ill again. It's a relapse, I'm afraid."

A relapse. What does that mean, a relapse?

"We're pretty certain she's got ME. There are lots of names for it but I like that one best. She can't go wearing herself out yet awhile. She'll have to take life more easily for some time. But she's only 11 – she's got plenty of time."

What does she mean, plenty of time?

Dr Draycott spends over an hour with me, examining me and asking questions and talking to me and mum. I've never met a doctor like her before.

She tries to explain what ME is. That's its short name. I can't pronounce the long one. And I don't really under-stand the explanation either – I was listening but I couldn't seem to remember what she said. I'll ask mum about it later.

"Will she be able to go to school?"

"Not for a while. She can have lessons at home, though. A teacher can come to the house."

"How long for?"

"It depends how quickly she gets strong again, but it may be quite a time. Patience is the name of the game. Later on, assuming she does go back, she oughtn't to do PE straight away. She'd better not stay in school for too long to start with, either. We don't want any more relapses. You might need to combine a bit of home tuition with occasional visits to school to see her friends, before she can get back there to attend lessons. Otherwise she could use all her energy just getting there. Then her brain won't remember what she's been taught. She shouldn't have to walk all the way there either. But don't worry about all that now – that's for the future. To start with she just needs to pace herself carefully and build up her strength. Health comes first."

"It sounds very complicated . . ." worries mum.

"Everyone's different," smiles Dr Draycott. "Don't worry, you'll soon get the hang of it. I'll ask someone from one of the patient organisations to contact you if you like – they can help you, they have documents you can give to the school so that the teachers understand. They're in touch with thousands of other families just like you – you can make friends, maybe share things like shopping, outings, looking after the children. You don't have to deal with this on your own. We can all work together – the school, Zoe, you, your GP – and me."

"Will I be able to do sports again?"

"Ah. The million dollar question."

I'm almost afraid to hear the answer. Every time I try to do sport I get ill. But I want to be a sportswoman. I love competing and it's wonderful to win.

"When I'm old enough, I want to win BBC Sports Personality of the Year," I say to the doctor. Then I'm afraid she's going to laugh.

She doesn't. But she smiles, though.

"You may well be able to do sport again. If you get really strong . . ."

She looks at me seriously.

"But – not for a long time?"

"Probably not, no. Your health is the most important thing, don't you think? Maybe you should consider a sport that's not too energetic."

I don't want to think about that one. I've always wanted to be a runner and I don't see that I can change my ambitions so easily. But I suppose she's right – there must be something else I can win at until I get back on the track. Snooker, perhaps. There aren't enough women snooker players, are there? There's a club in town that lets you join if an adult goes along. I can just see Gary's face when I do a 147 break.

"Mum, when I'm strong enough, can I join the snooker club?"

Mum stares at me. Dr Draycott laughs.

"I wish I'd thought of that instead of sitting behind my hospital desk. I could have been rich. But then, I really didn't have the talent."

She gets serious again.

"Take the long view, Zoe. Even standing at a snooker table is very tiring, there's a lot of bending and stooping, a lot of energy needed to break off – oh yes, I've had a go at it in my time too. And you have to have a lot of concentration. You really might have to find something else to do with that competitive instinct of yours in the meantime – and I don't mean sport."

At least she's being honest with me. That makes me feel better, it makes me feel adult. I need to start making my own decisions, not leave it all to the teachers and my mum.

"Think about something else you could do for now," she goes on. "It's really important for you to give yourself the best chance to get better – and it's always a good idea to watch out that you don't get a relapse – you may have to go on pacing yourself for quite some time." She looks at mum. "Everyone ought to do a bit of that really, shouldn't they? Not just people who are ill – lots of us burn the candle at both ends and it doesn't do us any good at all. Don't forget – Zoe can do a lot to make herself well again."

"How can it be up to Zoe whether she's ill or not?" asks mum.

"She can learn to let her body tell her what it can do. So, Zoe – rest properly, sleep when you need to and don't overdo things. I can recommend a good book for you and your mum to help you keep a diary. That will help you understand where you're going wrong, and what makes you worse again. In the end you'll begin to learn to control your energy scores instead of blowing all your energy in one go and having none left – that can make you feel dreadful, and that's no fun at all.

"When your body feels stronger, do just a little bit of gentle activity at a time, not too much. Stop before you get tired. And choose times when you feel able to manage it. That's the way to get better. Be patient and be kind to your body. It'll heal you all by itself if you keep enough energy to spare for the healing process. Will you do that?"

I promise her that I'll do as she says. Suddenly I want to cry. She's so kind.

I think of all the things I love to do and won't be able to

do for ages. Some of them I might never do again, perhaps. I feel as if I've lost myself.

But I've made a promise. I won't break it.

And I won't break my body either. I'll start taking care of it properly so that it can heal up, just like it does when I fall over and cut my knee.

I'll find something else I can win at too. There's got to be something.

I can still be me!

"It's a remarkable piece of writing and you certainly deserve to be our Young Writer of the Year. Congratulations!"

The famous television presenter leant forward. She handed Zoe a certificate and a notebook computer. The audience clapped and cheered.

Zoe glowed. She took the computer and stared at it as if it wasn't real.

"Thank you." It didn't seem enough just saying "Thank you", but she said it again anyway.

"It was such an original idea," went on the presenter. "And it taught us quite a lot."

"Really?"

"Oh yes. We didn't like your Mr Fisher though, that's until he turned into the hero."

Zoe laughed. "Mr Fisher's not his real name," she said. "I changed it for the story. He's been so understanding – I know it sounds a bit dramatic, but he saved my life."

In spite of her training, the presenter started, as if someone had pricked her with a pin. Surely – but no, the girl in front of her couldn't have ME herself? She looked perfectly all right. But if she did have ME – whatever had the TV researchers been doing to have missed this vital piece of information?

"We wondered how you managed to describe all the symptoms so well – we thought you must have known someone . . ." she searched for the right response.

"No, I knew because I have ME myself. I'm OK today, but sometimes I still need a wheelchair."

Zoe imagined millions of viewers all over the country, jolted into listening. The atmosphere in the studio had changed too.

"And the things that happened in your story?"

"They happened to me. All of them. And a lot more as well. It took ages to write the story because my brain kept refusing to think and I had to take a break. And it was hard to remember because it was 3 years ago and I was so ill at the time."

"You should have told us, Zoe."

"I know. But suppose everyone thought you'd only given me the prize because you felt sorry for me. It would be dreadful to win that way."

She looked round the studio.

"And none of you guessed, did you?"

"No, Zoe. We thought you must have a friend with ME." The presenter leaned over and put her hand on Zoe's arm. "You could have trusted us you know. Suppose you hadn't been able to come? We could have sent a car for you – saved you the journey on the train."

She was being very kind. She must be furious really. Zoe thought about the researcher she'd talked to on the phone.

"I haven't got anyone in trouble have I?"

"Hm. We'll have to think about that one . . ." she laughed. "But seriously, do you feel OK? Is there anything you need?" She seemed to have forgotten that they were on air. But presenters never forget they are on air.

Perhaps she knew more about ME than she was letting on, wanted the viewers to know too.

Zoe began to feel ashamed. If Lynne had been ill, she would have wanted to help. It would be awful if Lynne was ill and kept it a secret, didn't trust her.

"I suppose it was a bit silly. But we did drive here, so we didn't have all the hassle of the trains. It's not mum's fault either – I made her not say anything. I suppose I should have, in case I was ill in the studio."

"That's all right. We understand. Don't we, guys?"

The camera crew and the floor manager made all the right noises.

Zoe looked at them.

In that moment she made a decision.

"I shan't do it again. I won't ever pretend about it again. If I talk about my ME, maybe other children won't go through what I did, with no-one believing that they're ill. I didn't write about the worst of it – I did have a lot of people thinking I was making it up to get out of school. But I was lucky. We found a doctor who understood. Some children never get believed. Maybe I can really make a difference."

"Oh, I think you've already done that, Zoe," said the presenter.

Zoe could see out of the corner of her eye that a close-up of her face was on the monitor, being shown to millions.

"Really, I suppose I'm quite proud to be me. Does that sounds conceited?"

"Of course it doesn't. You should be proud. And I'm proud too, I'm very proud indeed that we chose you as our winner. Because that's what you are, Zoe, isn't it folks? One of life's winners."

# A Personal Message to all Young People With ME

## Zoe's Story – who is it for?

Zoe's story has been written for you, your friends, your family and your teachers, who all need to understand about your illness.

Zoe has her own personality, and her own ambitions. She especially likes to compete. Her ambition is to be a professional sportsperson.

When Zoe gets ME, she has to find a way to save enough energy for her body to heal itself, without losing the essence of who she is. That isn't an easy challenge, and she has to change her lifestyle to meet it.

Like Zoe, people who get ME usually find that they can no longer do the things they used to do. When they try to "get back to normal" too soon, before their bodies have healed sufficiently, they just relapse – that means they get worse all over again.

This can be frightening and very depressing. It may have happened to you. Some people no longer feel like the same person they used to be. Who is this person who used to be good at maths? – or writing, or sports, or whatever – they may ask themselves.

The answer is really very simple. Someone with ME is still the same person as before – but they are also a new person at the same time.

_Just like everyone else, you are a mixture of all the things that have happened to you in the past, plus the things that are happening to you now._

## Accepting what has happened

Usually we don't notice ourselves changing and developing as new experiences are added to old ones bit by bit, day by day. But when big changes happen suddenly, as they can do when we get ill, it's all a bit too quick to handle and we don't feel like ourselves any more.

People often react to this by refusing to accept what has happened at all. They may just keep on relapsing and relapsing because as soon as their symptoms go away they try to be exactly the same person they were before they got ME.

When they relapse, they often go to bed and rest, so eventually their body starts to recover – but then they go straight back to their old lives again and have yet another relapse.

In America, these relapses are called "flares", meaning a "flare-up" of symptoms. I think it is a very good expression as that is exactly what happens.

Why do people behave like this? Why do they keep on

making themselves worse the moment they feel better?

_Because they don't like the changes in themselves, they try to pretend that these changes just aren't there._

## How can changing your lifestyle help?

When people have ME, they need to change their lifestyle to help their bodies save some energy to heal and get strong again.

Until people have come to terms with what has happened to them, they can't begin to change their lifestyle – because they haven't yet accepted that it's necessary. So they get stuck in an "up and down" lifestyle – either they are feeling "up" or "down" and they don't really stabilise somewhere in the middle.

Changing your lifestyle to one that will help you get better needs lots of thought, and you will need help from your family and others to work out what is best for you. Zoe has school lessons at home for a while and learns to change the amount of energy she uses.

Adapting and pacing life carefully gives a person with ME the best chance to get strong and well again.

This book contains information for your doctors and teachers to help them help you with this.

*In the end, it is within your own control to help your body to heal itself.*

## Nicer people

We are all a mixture of our past and our present. Whether it is illness, or the job we end up doing, or the people we are friends with, or the places we visit – we all change and develop.

Many people with ME, through learning to adapt in order to get strong and well again, say that they have become much nicer people, more patient with others who are ill or have difficulties of one sort or another.

Illness is a horrible experience, and ME is a horrible illness. You may think that you are the only person who is going through this. Far from it. All of us who have been where you are now, know what you are going through.

*And all of us want to help you.*

## You are not alone

There are thousands of other young people all over the world, many of them in this country, who are experiencing exactly the same thing as you. It may be a good idea to contact some of them.

You will soon make new friends this way – friends whom you don't have to explain anything to. You won't have to say: "I might be able to come and see you on Saturday – but I might not if I wake up and find I'm having a bad day." They will know that already.

You might find that many of these young people live a long way from you, but this means you can build up a network of friends to write to, talk to on the phone and exchange emails with.

Looking to the future, you will have many more friends than those around you, and they will be spread all over this country, maybe all over the world.

*Many well people never build up a friendship network like this.*

## Family contacts

Some families whose children have ME truly bless the day when they got in touch with others in the same position.

If they find another family nearby, they can share all sorts of practical tasks like shopping, keeping one another company, looking after one another's interests generally. And of course, they can share outings and special occasions too.

Some doctors used to think that if people with ME talked too much to other people with ME, they would all continue to be ill.

Maybe these doctors feared that being ill together was some kind of positive group experience, like being part of a club, the problem being that this club would chuck you out if you got well again.

They may also have feared that everyone in the group would just depress everyone else with lists of their own symptoms, and that would make them ill for longer too.

**_If you look at these two ideas, they actually contradict one another._**

## How do these ideas contradict one another?

Going to see others with ME can't be enjoyable and also depressing at the same time, can it? So why did doctors get so worried and advise their patients not to seek support from patient organisations?

The idea came from research which seemed to show that people who had contact with support groups stayed ill for longer. Of course they did – they were more ill to start with and that's why they went to the support groups! So that argument was soon shown to be untrue. It was what is called an "artefact" of the research itself – something that did not exist in reality.

I think that most of us who have been through the worst of ME would be able to reassure doctors that having ME is not fun. It is not something we would willingly experience just to make friends. If we do make new friends, we can always stay in contact with them whether we continue to be ill or not.

And the depression? Certainly you may feel very depressed at times. Anyone with a long-lasting and disabling illness gets depressed at times – they wouldn't be normal if they didn't. Many young people with ME feel useless. They feel that because they need things done for them all the time, they can offer nothing back.

*This is not true.*

## What you can offer

If you contact other young people with ME, you may find that you can offer them friendship in a way which they have not experienced before.

Perhaps their well friends haven't understood that they are really ill. Perhaps they have been bullied or maybe no-one has stayed in contact with them when they have been stuck at home.

Maybe they have bouts of crying – this can happen in ME, especially if you get too tired and push yourself too hard. The distress you feel seems to be something to do with the effects of ME on the levels of brain chemicals. The crying tends to pass in an hour or two, but when you're going through it you can wonder if it will ever stop.

A short message to people who are going through a bad patch can do wonders.

*You can send cards to the Young Action Online office for us to forward to someone else who needs cheering up. See Young Action Online page 51.*

## Success

The story of Zoe is the story of a young person going through a nasty case of ME. There are cases of ME which are not as bad as Zoe's but there are also cases which are worse.

Zoe is someone who has a very strong competitive instinct – she wants to win at something and when she finds she isn't well enough to do sports, she finds something new to win at.

But winning isn't what everyone wants to do. Getting good exam results, having friends, enjoying life generally – young people have all sorts of different priorities, and these must be respected. You are unique and so are your hopes and fears.

School plays a central role in the lives of most young people. But it is easy to feel like a failure if you can't achieve what you used to be able to achieve. Remember that there will be something you can succeed at.

Schools are very exhausting places – they are academic hothouses and relapses are common in young people with ME who go back to school too soon. They commonly find that they use all their energy just getting there and walking around the building and then they can't think properly and get poor academic results.

Often they can get much better academic results by learning at home, either through home tuition or through a distance learning course. The world is changing fast, and there are lots of new schemes springing up to teach sick children at home via the Internet, phone, post and fax.

It is not your fault if you can't fit into the school system. It has been set up for young people who are fit and well. If you are not fit and well, it is the school's job to change the system to help you and it is your legal right to receive education that is suitable for your needs.

*You can still keep contact with school in order to see friends.*

## Going back to school

Many children and young people with ME do go back to school again – at first part-time, and eventually full-time when they are well.

Others don't – they find the home learning situation keeps them in better health and they no longer get relapses. It all depends on the case.

In Australia it is quite normal not to go to school, because the country is so huge that families are spread out all over the outback and just can't get to a school. A research study found that these young people actually got better academic results than the pupils who went to school!

Just getting a lot better is an achievement in itself. Some young people want to concentrate on that and don't mind if their education has to take a back seat for a while. Others care so much about getting qualifications that this is more important to them even than getting better.

Remember that, as in Australia, getting educated and getting to school are not the same thing. You may be able to get educated and get better at the same time if you organise your life correctly.

Everyone has their own priorities. Each young person's life and ambitions are unique and should be respected.

You have to be educated by law. But in the end, try to put your health first. Studies have shown that this is what families want most for their children, even more than success in education or anything else. They are probably right.

*Your future success can be enhanced by having the right contacts to help you. Young Action Online specialises in giving you the right contacts.*

# Young Action Online

*(and no, you don't have to be connected to the Internet!)*

*Free services available by phone, post, email and on the YAOnline website.*

## How did it all start?

In 1997, Children in Need gave the national charity Action for ME special funding for children and young people and I became their Children's Officer.

I set up a Children's Department at Action for ME, which became the ME charity listed in "Supporting Pupils with Medical Needs - a good practice guide", issued by the government Department of Health and the Department for Education and Employment. Education Authorities, doctors and other professionals as well as young people and their families regularly ask for help.

I now run *Young Action Online*, a free support system for all young people with ME. The heart of *Young Action Online* is a free website which contains a library of documents that you can download and use free of charge.

The documents there are useful for young people with ME and also for teachers, school doctors, your family, your MP, journalists – anyone you think ought to know about ME.

You can take as many copies as you like. Many of the documents are by specialist doctors and you may therefore like to give some of them to your own doctor.

*If you do not have access to the Internet you can order print-outs of the documents and also the website pages.*

## The Young Action Online website is at:

http://www.jafc.demon.co.uk/yaonline/

The site is updated monthly and has many different pages as well as the documents library, including:

- The News Page
- Jane Colby's Secret Diary (the Inside Story of the Children's Department)
- Roll of Honour
- "Sebastian Says"

Sebastian the website Spider OGW (Order of the Golden Web) has a heart of gold, though at times he can be a little trying. As resident poet and celebrity on the website, he describes himself as "the best poet in the world – and also the most modest". Hm. He is always exchanging emails with Toad of Toad Hall and is really rather like him in many ways.

Between you and me, I have a deal of trouble keeping Seb in hand at times, as he tends to get into a Virtual Huff if he isn't allowed to write my Secret Diary. I am hoping he has not noticed this sentence or there may be trouble later . . .

## What else can you get from YAOnline?

- *Free Welcome Pack* including a copy of the TYMES magazine, which is recommended by ME special ist and medical author Dr Darrel Ho-Yen.

- *Free seasonal Info/Action Packs*. You receive these quarterly.

- *Open Network*: professionals. A postal list of professionals who can advise you and your family direct. There are doctors, careers advisers, educational psychologists, exams officers, home tutors, lawyers etc.

- *Open Network*: young people. You can register your own details on the Open Network too, if you would like other young people with ME to write to you.

- *You won't be forgotten* on your birthday or at Christmas either.

*You can also contribute to the work by sending in Christmas cards or Well-Wishing Cards to be passed on to other young people who are going through a bad patch.*

53

## AND

## You can nominate people for

## The Roll of Honour

On the website is a Roll of Honour for which you can nominate helpful friends, doctors, teachers or even your mum.

The people you nominate will be sent a specially designed certificate to display. It will show their name in calligraphy by Yvonne Arber and will be signed by YAOnline President Martin Arber, former Chairman of Action for ME.

*Don't forget to thank the people who have helped you most. Nominate them by post, enclosing 6 2nd class stamps per nomination, to cover costs.*

"Online" doesn't just mean connected to the Internet. It means connected to all the support we can give.

## To register:

Write to
Young Action Online, PO Box 4347, Stock, Ingatestone, CM4 9TE

Or:
Email the form you will find on the website

# PART 2

# Do you teach a young person with ME?

## A GIRL LIKE ME

*A girl lies in bed all day,*
*Wishing she could run and play*
*Her face is white as teardrops fall*
*Still she can do nothing at all.*

*Her Mum was a gift from above*
*Looked after her and gave her love*
*She had a cousin who was just the best*
*Who understood more than the rest.*

*Her friends she had were really great too,*
*But couldn't quite understand what she was going through*
*She longs once more to be like you*
*To go to school and hobbies too*

*I know how she feels, I can quite often see*
*For the girl is quite a lot like me.*

Heather McLean
when aged 12

"I have taught many ME pupils over the past few years. In general they are rewarding to teach as they are often intelligent and keen to learn. They do have their frustrations, but I have been lucky enough to see some of them come through the disease

56

and go on to achieve G.C.S.E.'s, A levels, etc.

I have found it generally unproductive to push too hard for work to be completed on time for school – although the schools do not always understand this."

Home Tutor responding to Action for ME Questionnaire

Teaching children with ME is a specialised job and yet one of the most successful cases I have come across involved a 10-year old boy in a school where the head teacher had not even heard of the disease. He did not know that it is a neurological disease affecting both the brain and the body. He did not know that it is commonly triggered by a virus and may even be a relation of poliomyelitis. He simply followed the cardinal rule; he believed the child.

Over several years his young pupil progressed through many stages, all of which the head teacher facilitated and supervised. From being ill at home and unable to work at all, he came through the stage of having a home tutor and began visiting school each week for a one-hour lesson with his home tutor in the head's office. After this he became able to attend school, at first part-time and finally full-time, but without undertaking physical education. The last I heard, he was beginning to do a little swimming and other physical activities. All this was possible because he was allowed to heal at the rate his own body dictated.

Some children become seriously ill with ME and cannot receive tuition for a long time. Many recover sufficiently to attend school, but others do not, often because they develop ME in their teens and reach school leaving age before becoming strong enough. There are also those whose brain function is so severely affected that the energy expended on attending school depletes their concentration to an extent where academic achievement becomes impossible in that situation. Each case is different, but one thing remains constant; the knowledge, skill and attitude of the teacher can make or break both the pupil's health and sense of self-worth.

Wherever you are teaching your pupil – at home, in school, or in a small unit – there are simple practical tips which, if employed, should enable your pupil to achieve without becoming more ill in the process.

Yours is a huge responsibility but one which, like the head teacher above, you can readily meet if you simply "observe the patient", as all doctors are exhorted to do, and act accordingly. You can be sure that your pupil and indeed the whole family will value you not only as a teacher but as a friend, and will remember you with gratitude and affection for the rest of their lives.

*See:*     *Real Examples; Educational Modifications. A Young Action Online document. Pupils recall teachers and schools and the help they gave.*

## Energy

Someone with ME is like a mobile phone. When a mobile phone runs out of charge it looks exactly the same on the outside but, as anyone knows who has forgotten to recharge this infuriating tool of modern life, the thing then refuses to work – until, of course, we charge it up again.

In just the same way, the body and the brain of someone with ME often seem to run out of charge. Unlike others, we cannot sit down with a cup of tea for half an hour and feel fine again. Not even a night's sleep will re-charge us. So we have to eke out what energy we have, spending it thoughtfully as if it were hard-earned cash. Dr Darrel Ho-Yen's book *Better Recovery from Viral Illnesses* goes into this in detail; the whole concept of regarding energy as money to be conserved and spent with care came from his pen.

It is vital for teachers to realise the scale of energy depletion we are talking about. In my earlier book *ME – The New Plague* described the experience of running on empty and its consequences as follows:

*The essential point to grasp is this; the effect of making an effort in ME is out of all proportion to the effort made . . . one seems to be operating on another planet with many times the gravity of earth.*

Zoe Williams, a young adult with ME, describes eating an apple. "Eating is a big activity if you have ME fairly severely," she says.

## EATING AN APPLE
### Zoe K Williams

*crunch   chrunch chrunch   crunch crunch   crunch crunch   gulp*
*crunch crunch crunch crunch crunch crunch gulp*
*crunch... crunch... crunch... crunch... crunch... gulp*

*sigh*

*crunch...   crunch...   crunch...   crunch...   crunch...   crunch...*
*crunch... gulp*

*How much apple is there in an apple?*

*crunch.... crunch.... crunch.... crunch.... crunch....*
*crunch.... gulp*
*rest*

*crunch.. crunch.. crunch.. crunch.. crunch.. gulp*
*etc.*

*Quite a lot.*
*Save the rest for later.*

Substitute work for the apple, and here is the perfect model for teaching a child with ME. Number-crunching and word-crunching are just as exhausting as eating.

How much lesson is there in a lesson? Quite a lot. Save the rest for later.

## Practical hints and tips

When Ben Broke-Smith was thirteen, I became involved in making recommendations for his education. I soon realised that some of the hints and tips I was at that time compiling for use in my lectures would be best compiled by Ben himself and his mother. This is the list they came up with.

### PLEASE

*Speak slowly and be patient*
*Keep explanations simple*
*Pause and wait for my response*
*Don't speak while I'm thinking*
*Minimise processes to complete work*
*Let me help control the pace of work*
*Stop the moment I need a break*
*Ask my energy level, not how I feel*
*Help me make the best of life*
*Let me use energy-saving aids*
*Listen when I try to explain.*

Each of these points has a ready explanation:

- Speaking too fast causes a person with ME to hear each word without being able to process it into a sentence. The whole thing sounds like a foreign language.

- Long complicated explanations cannot be followed – the short term memory can be so damaged that only a few words can be retained at a time.

- The child with ME will take a while to work out what you

61

said, and then work out a response. If you speak during this process, the thread is lost.

- Processes like brain-storming, drafting and finally producing a finished piece of writing are too exhausting for many children with ME and both their health and the quality of the work will suffer unless the processes required are reduced to a minimum. Course-work also needs to be minimised.

- Giving some control to the young person is the best way to work within the limits of the illness without pro-voking too many symptoms, though some symptoms will probably be unavoidable during or after periods of concentration. Some pupils may, paradoxically, know that they are beginning to feel ill but may continue working out of a misguided determination to "push through the pain". Occasionally, they may get away with it but it is not advisable.

- If your pupil says it's time to stop, it is. Instantly. To be tempted to carry on, even for another five minutes, is to invite a very nasty downturn and a possible delay of days or even weeks before return to the former level of capability. If the pupil becomes very pale or com-plains of feeling ill, stop straight away and suggest a snack and a drink; something sweet may help, as low blood sugar episodes are common in ME and people really do need to eat immediately.

- Asking "How are you?" poses a dilemma to a long term sick child. Does he answer "Fine", which, whilst untrue, is short and easy (but risks giving the wrong impression) or does he say "Awful" and exhaust himself reeling off a list of the most depressing symptoms. Better to ask "What's your energy level?" Use a system you are both happy with to assess this. Schemes for grading energy typically suggest 10 levels. Your pupil's level 10 could equal "fit as a flea and able to play football" and level 1 could equal "lying in bed in pain and unable to have my lesson". Or if this is too depressing because level 10 seems unattainable, level 10 could be set at "able to work well for the whole lesson" and level 1 could equal "able to work for only a few minutes at a time". The exact scale you use doesn't really matter, so long as you both know what you mean. In practice you are unlikely to need 10 levels – 5 is far simpler and quite adequate for your purpose. Or just use words: "really grotty, partly grotty, hardly grotty at all" would do – and might just raise a smile. Remember, though, that the grade "hardly grotty at all" applies only to the present situation. If your pupil is at home, "hardly grotty at all" could soon turn into "really grotty" in another situation.

- Helping a young person with ME to make the best of life means accepting the illness for what it is and not regarding life with ME as the most terrible example of doom and gloom that it is possible to imagine. Do smile, do allow "sick" jokes – black humour about one's own illness is common amongst people with ME and although laughter may be exhausting it is healing too. A life consisting of nothing but pain, illness and a struggle to complete the simplest piece of work may seem hardly worth living, even for an adult. If someone reports seeing your pupil "out on his bike", remember that some enjoyment is necessary for life with ME to be bearable, even if it means paying for it later. Your pupil needs to come to terms with this condition and to test its boundaries from time to time. Perhaps that

ride on the bike will reveal that more can now be attempted
without too many after-effects. On the other hand it may
reveal a clear need for more caution. It is part of the learning
process and just as important as any other work.

- Energy-saving aids include: worksheets and word-
  processing to minimise manual writing, since this may be
  painful and some pupils become dyslexic for a time; CD
  Roms, talking books and various audio-visual material;
  allowing the pupil to email or fax finished work from home
  rather than having to complete it all at once in a lesson.
  Some pupils need to follow distance learning courses from
  specialist providers who also offer personal tutors; contact
  may be made by phone, fax, email or home visit. Provision
  of technological aids can be a life-saver.

- Ben's last point is perhaps the most important of all.
  "Listening to the child" is the counterpart of "observing the
  patient". Believing what we hear is the glue which holds the
  whole process together.

## Living with ME

Children with ME typically suffer from severe headache and
generalised pain which is not amenable to painkillers. The
brain's perception of pain in the body is disordered and some
children will cry out if touched. They may also have odd sensa-
tions such as burning skin or pins and needles, or a feeling that
insects are running over them. Their muscles may twitch. All
these neurological signs and symptoms can be frightening as
well as hard to bear and the spirit of endurance shown by these
youngsters demands our greatest respect.

## STREETS OF PAIN

*As I was walking down the streets of pain*
*I was scared and quite unprepared for what might*
  *happen to me.*
*Then I saw a face appear from my innermost fears*
*and this is what it said to me.*
*Turn that frown upside down*
*to create the perfect smile*
*Because if God wanted you to frown*
*he would have made your lips upside down.*

Natalie Powers
when aged 13

In such a situation, friends and family are desperately needed: family, to give care and security; friends to give contact with others of the same age and with the outside world. Whilst it can be helpful to have friends in the same position as oneself, it is good to keep contact with those who are not ill and to develop interests, if possible, that have nothing to do with one's own illness.

Children with ME can find themselves forgotten, isolated, shunned even. Schools can help prevent this by teaching other pupils about the illness and by keeping contact through written notes, telephone messages and visits. Answers to notes may not be possible, however, and the pupil may be unable to talk on the phone for long (or at all). Visits should be short; one or two people dropping in from time to time is better than a whole group just once.

Contact is much more easily initiated by the fit and well, rather than by the sick pupil and such efforts earn serious numbers of brownie points. Karen Cambray, when aged fifteen, explained: "This poem is dedicated to my friends, Amy, Sally, Lucy, Nicola, Thara, Katherine and Kim. For all the support they've given me."

> *I want you to know*
> *how much I appreciate*
> *each moment you thought of me.*
> *I know it must be hard for you*
> *I know it is for me.*
> *I wanted to give something back to you*
> *for all you've done for me.*
> *I want to say, 'Thank you,' for caring about me.*
> *When times were hard and things were rough*
> *you were always there.*
> *I knew I could talk and you would listen*
> *to what I had to say.*
> *I will never forget you.*

*See: Your ME Assembly. This is a Young Action Online information pack. Containing ohps and Karen's poems. For use by teachers and pupils.*

It comes very hard to see life slipping past without you. Much has been made of the role which depression plays in ME, and people with ME do sometimes have bouts of distress which can be hard to live through due to abnormalities in the balance of brain chemicals. But it would be a very odd person who had an illness like this and did not suffer some depression.

## HOW I FEEL

*I sit around all day
watching children run and play,
that was once me I say.*

*I see the sun rise up then fall
But still I've not been out at all.*

*I want my old life back,
To sing and dance and laugh
These things that I lack.*

*But my flower has closed
This darkness has imposed
Why can't I just be well?*

*People don't see what it's doing to me
I want to have fun to run and be free.*

*I want to be out, part of God's creation,
Part of the world
Part of the nation.*

*I see these things through pains of glass.*

*My world's inside a window
I see lots of people walk about
I'm trapped — won't someone let me out?*

Heather McLean
when aged 12

It would also be easy to develop a sense of uselessness and failure, but as the home tutor quoted above has noted, pupils with ME are generally keen to learn and do not easily give up on their hopes. They may have very poor memory, however, in which case subjects such as art and poetry can be excellent sources both of expression and real achievement. Motivation to attain a high standard is strong once we show that we believe in their ability.

When you have to spend long periods tied to one room and your view of the world is the view out of your window, natural beauty is not only soothing but becomes a source of wonder and acute observation; these young people have time to look closely at things others take for granted.

We may be concerned with the business of teaching them, but they also have the ability to teach us about our world and to help us see it with fresh eyes.

## THE ROSES

*The roses stand*
*Tall and bright*
*Shining in the sunlight.*
*Smell the scent*
*Of the lovely flowers*
*Pink and red all pretty colours.*
*The bees come for food*
*While inside the flower moves*
*Pollen rubs upon his side, and so he*
*Spreads the pollen wide.*

Victoria Western
when aged 8

There are many young writers out there every bit as talented as the Zoe of our story. One of them even goes by the same name. What better way to end this section than by letting her tell us just what it means to endure this disease and to grow through it into a philosopher and poet.

### GEORGE'S FIELD

Zoe K Williams
On seeing the countryside for the first time in 15 months

*I see a kestrel hovering so still*
*I thought it was a speck on my glasses.*
*Rabbits, moving so fast*
*my eyes can't keep up.*

*The downs are five miles away from here.*
*Two thousand times the distance*
*from my bed to the wall.*
*No wonder it seems so vast.*

*Are the hills and trees really there?*
*Am I actually seeing them with my own eyes?*
*Nothing but air between us?*
*It seems impossible.*

*Trevor thought I might be disappointed*
*in the real world -*
*Good photos look so impressive,*
*better than the real thing.*

69

*Yet this is beyond my imaginings,*
*perhaps I dream in 2D.*
*Windows take away half*
*of the third dimension.*

*Three stars come out*
*adding even greater distance*
*and another dimension.*
*Looking back in time, viewing eternity.*

# Key information for the guidance of doctors and teachers

In 1997, the largest study of ME to date was published, causing a furore in the medical press. The study investigated the pattern of ME in British schools and revealed statistics so huge that they found their way onto the front page of the Guardian newspaper under the headline *Schools hit by ME Plague.*

Dr Elizabeth Dowsett, a renowned ME expert, had approached me in 1991 because she had been given details of an outbreak of ME in a village school following an epidemic of gastro-enteritis. She wanted to know what was happening country-wide.

Our 5-year study involved collecting statistics from a school roll of over 333,000 UK pupils and 27,000 school staff. Major findings included the following:

- *51% of pupils on Long Term Sickness Absence from school were suffering from ME. This far exceeded the figures for any other illness; cancer and leukaemia, at 23%, formed the next largest category.*
- *39% of cases occurred in clusters of both staff and pupils. A further 21% occurred in pairs. In Japan, a pair has been defined as a cluster; had we included pairs in our own cluster figures, this would have meant that a total of 60% of cases were in clusters. The pattern observed was consistent with a condition initiated by infection.*

In the year 2000, three years after the publication of this study, the only serious attempts to modify education for pupils with ME in order that they may access learning and achieve success have been limited to local initiatives. No national policy exists for the education of these children. As a result, misperception of the nature of the disease in educational institutions has caused many children to relapse in attempting to attend school. We are making our children sicker in the name of education.

As a former head teacher, I am the first to admit that health must come first. Educational issues (i.e. school attendance, National Curriculum requirements, examinations, special educational needs) frequently trigger disputes between LEAs and families, into which doctors are drawn. Sometimes these disputes even lead to case conferences and child protection proceedings, with some parents being labelled as having Munchausen's Syndrome by Proxy, a rare condition where someone harms another person in order to gain attention for themselves.

The BBC *Panorama* programme of November 1999 highlighted this problem. The BBC health correspondent Matthew Hill and I collaborated to devise a questionnaire which was sent to all the families in Young Action Online.

The response rate was 62%, and the statistics as reported by the BBC revealed that:

- *59% of families were told by doctors that their children's illness was caused by psychological problems*
- *5% had undergone psychological treatment. Their parents all reported it either had no effect or made their children worse*
- *7% of children from families questioned had been subject to child protection proceedings (i.e. court proceedings either threatened or carried out).*
- *15% of families were told that it was their psychological problems that were causing the child's illness.*
- *A high proportion of parents, 4%, were branded with Munchausen's Syndrome by Proxy (MSBP). This represents one in 18 families surveyed. (National Statistics show the*

*syndrome affects just one in 100,000 families.)*

If these statistics are representative, then out of every 100 families whose children contract ME, 7 will be threatened with having their child taken into care and 4 will be thought to have MSBP. In order for this situation to improve, doctors, teachers and parents will need to collaborate in caring compassionately for the sick child, putting aside out of date perceptions of ME, believing what the child says, and allowing the child/young person some say in the management of what is, after all, their own life.

**The Management of ME in children**

Managing a case of childhood ME is not the same as managing an adult case, because children have to be educated by law and inappropriate educational methods can undermine the doctor's management. However, good educational management can be combined with good medical management so that they become two sides of the same coin.

Academic success, so far as health and ability permits, can thereby be achieved without provoking further deterioration in the child's condition. This gives an enormous boost to confidence and self-esteem and also helps the child obtain qualifications for the future.

*The Collaborative Care Management Model*

GP Tutor Dr Nigel Hunt and I, in my capacity of Children's Officer with Action for ME, designed this model jointly. It is simple in concept and has been found to work well. Sarah Gill, the teenage girl whose case formed the basis of the development of the model, obtained a Grade B in her GCSE despite serious illness and disability. The report is to be found on the Young Action Online website at:

http://www.jafc.demon.co.uk/yaonline/

The key part of the Model, which identifies the child as the Client, is an Action Framework for General Practitioners which acts as a useful check-list.

*The Action Framework*

1  Diagnose (either by GP or through referral) as promptly as possible, to free up the family's access to support from various agencies.
2  Inform the family of relevant benefits and practical support available.
3  Maintain regular contact with family to monitor health of child and treat symptoms as appropriate.
4  Give details of preferred patient organisations to the family.
5  Identify child's learning status (does attendance at school exacerbate illness?) and long-term aims.
6  Liaise with LEA/school to set up learning programme which will help to achieve these aims without endangering health.

*NB There is no legal requirement to attend school; social contact can be provided for separately. Modern technology is resulting in the proliferation of distance learning facilities.*

It would be a serious omission for me not to comment here on the role of psychiatrists in the treatment of ME, now often called Chronic Fatigue Syndrome. CFS is an umbrella term which was identified by the National ME Task Force (Westcare) as combining the neurological disease of ME with other fatigue-inducing conditions.

This is a controversial area, with psychiatric treatment often being applied to children. Cognitive Behaviour Therapy and graded exercise, often favoured by psychiatrists, may have their place in helping some people with certain kinds of fatigue illnesses, but many children with typical cases of ME, according to both them and their parents, have been made far worse, and families are beginning to take cases to court and seek publicity for their plight. There is a divide in the medical profession as to the efficacy and safety of this method of treating ME.

The idea that ME is a psychological condition has been largely disproved by the great number of physical abnormalities found in the brains and bodies of these patients. If we look back a few years, Winter Vomiting Disease, which was labelled during one particular outbreak as mass hysteria, is now known to be caused by the Norwalk Virus. In the 21st century, it is surely time to learn from such mistakes.

Early investigation of every childhood case of ME would assist us greatly in identifying any viruses which may have triggered it.

**A New Teacher's Code**

Sadly, if I analyse the reasons why children with ME and their parents ask for help, virtually 100% of those with whom I have dealt personally have been disbelieved by someone, somewhere along the line. Usually this has come from a doctor, teacher or other professional but sometimes from a member of their own family, or even from all three.

*The reasons for disbelief are usually:*

- The physical signs of their illness (e.g. pallor, shaking or shivering, unsteady gait, clumsiness, twitching muscles,

75

vacant expression reminiscent of petit mal etc.) have not been closely enough observed.

- Their own descriptions of how they feel (too hot in a cold atmosphere, too cold in a hot atmosphere, nausea, pain, weakness, malaise etc) have not been given sufficient attention, with some children being told that they are not really in pain at all.
- Their explanations of things which happen to their bodies when they do too much (heart palpitations, exhaustion to the point of collapse, inability to understand what is said, difficulty speaking or remembering words, faintness, numbness etc.) have been given little credence or put down to psychological factors.

Children are in a very vulnerable position when they leave their homes for a day at school. They depend on teachers for their well-being as well as their education. Teachers can often help by the simplest of actions. It is important to remember, for example, that emotional distress is often an early sign of exhaustion and can be alleviated by a rest, whereas shakiness, disorientation and malaise is often a sign of low blood sugar and can be alleviated by a snack.

Far from being psychological, the child's symptoms are indicative of various malfunctions. These malfunctions can lead the unwary into danger; for a teacher to insist on physical education, for example, is unwise as it can not only cause relapse but can affect the heart during certain stages of the illness. We know, for example, that exercising hard with influenza can lead to heart attack.

I would like to use this book as an opportunity to launch a simple code for teachers of children with ME, who are often in direct contact with children in key situations where these signs and symptoms manifest themselves:

## OBSERVE
## LISTEN
## BELIEVE

**Key principles for teachers to remember are:**

- *The full National Curriculum is not a suitable programme for children and students with ME. Because of cognitive disturbance including, very often, severe memory malfunction, children with ME in general cannot study many subjects at one time without detracting from success and also, in many cases, exacerbating their illness.*
- *Content of courses needs to be minimised. The student's memory and store of energy are not, in general, sufficient to enable them to follow the full course.*
- *Examinations need to be tailored to the requirements of the illness. The maximum amount of the students' energy needs to be utilised for the examination in order to achieve the best grade possible; therefore they often need to avoid travel and take the exam at home, they need rest/food breaks and extra time, and sometimes an amanuensis who can write for them or the use of a keyboard, since manual writing can be painful and physically difficult. The examination should be scheduled for the time of day when their brain is at maximum arousal, typically the afternoon.*

Children with ME are not only unwell, they also have Special Educational Needs by virtue of the brain dysfunction inherent in the condition. The Special Educational Needs Co-ordinator needs to be aware of their difficulties and an Individual Education Plan should be established. The school medical service can also offer invaluable support.

Arrangements such as those above can be personalised to fit

the individual case and will help greatly to level the playing field for children whose illness severely disadvantages them through no fault of their own. We must not fail them.

The last word should perhaps go to the doctors and teachers who have recommended and used these methods and, of course, to the families who are in receipt of them. The overwhelming verdict given in letters, emails, phone calls and meetings is that they are practical and affordable. And they work.

Note: The specific principles of Energy Efficient Education which the author has been developing are due for publication in the year 2000 in the book *Child Power, Succeeding with ME*, to be published by Dome Vision.

By the same author

# Books

*ME – The New Plague*
This book kills the myth that ME is "all in the mind", investigates the link between ME and polio, and shows how we are failing our children as we did in the polio years. Essential both for the professional and the layman; designed to be easily read by those with ME and contains a Survivors' Lifestyle Checklist.
ISBN 1 8608 3215 6 First and Best in Education Ltd.

*He Hit Me First*
What makes a bully tick? Can a bully be changed? Designed as a practical teacher training manual with thought-provoking exercises for pupils and staff, this publication shows how to overcome bullying in primary schools.
ISBN 1 86083 113 3 First and Best in Education Ltd.

## Studies and papers (selection only)

*10 Points on organising ME care for children*
Information for GPs tabulated into ten key issues and their solutions. GP Magazine July 9 1999 p 70

*The School Child With ME*
First article on ME and its educational management in this specialist publication. It is still the definitive article to present as evidence for the necessity of special provision. British Journal of Special Education March 1994 vol 21 no 1 pp 9-11

*Long Term Sickness Absence due to ME/CFS in UK schools; an epidemiological study with medical and educational implications.*
Largest study of ME to date (333,024 pupils, 27,327 staff) Reveals that ME is the biggest cause of long term sickness absence from school. Also uncovers new evidence for an infective origin for this disease. Dowsett EG, Colby J Journal of Chronic Fatigue Syndrome May 1997 vol 3 (2) pp 29-42

*Taking ME Seriously*
Children with ME and its implications for their education.
Special Children magazine May 1996 vol 93 pp 18-20

*Polio 'link' may alter teaching of ME children*
Article drawing together some of the issues discussed in the book *ME – The New Plague*. The Sunday Times (Education Pages) 30th June 1996

*Focusing on Children*
How schools can respond to individual needs using ME-friendly principles. The

CFIDS Chronicle January/February 1998 pp 36-37

**Students and ME**
The particular needs of students and institutions. Newscheck (pub. by NASEN) November 1994 vol 5 No 2 pp 7-8

*Learning is hard when you're too weak to eat*
The argument for special provision for children with ME. The Independent [Education +] 22nd May 1997

**Feature articles in the TYMES Magazine (The Young ME Sufferer) including:**

*Getting a Life*
Why psychiatric treatment has been forced on children with ME. TYMES Issue 26 Autumn 1998 pp 7-8
*Britain is e-mail capital of Europe* Usefulness of the Internet for young people with ME. TYMES Issue 27 Winter 1999 (Internet Special) pp 8-9
*Follow the Yellow Brick Road* Finding a personal path and achieving goals without threatening health. TYMES Issue 29 Summer 1999 (Aims and Ambitions Special) pp 6-7

Contact TYMES at 9 Patching Hall Lane, Chelmsford, Essex, CM1 4DH.

**And:**

*The ME Library*
Situated at Young Action Online. Print-outs are available.
http://www.jafc.demon.co.uk/yaonline/
An expanding collection of documents for young people with ME, their families and professionals. Some documents below were written jointly with other specialists.

*The library includes:*
*Energy Efficient Education: main principles*
*The Collaborative Care Management Model* (with Action Framework for GPs)
*Quick Guide to the Long Term Sickness Absence Survey* (main statistics)
*Guidelines for Schools*
*The Children's Charter*
*ME and Learning: problems and solutions*
*Social Services and Children with ME*
*Does ME Cluster in Schools?*
*Diet in ME: is it such a big deal?*
*Students and ME*
*School Examinations and ME*
*Graded exercise: does it really work?*
*Educational modifications: real examples*
*Childhood ME* (a multi-authored report with medical and educational sections)